A Study of "Good" Microbes

A Small Essay for Notice

By Michael Reed

A Study of "Good" Microbes

A Small Essay for Notice

By Michael Reed

Acknowledgement

I want to thank God for giving me the interest on this subject.

Table of Contents

Introduction

Many kinds of microorganisms are some of the fascinating creatures on Earth. Many species were made to produce various functions for us and the environment. Most species can break down complex matter into simple compounds for other creatures to live. Some species use photosynthesis to turn gas into compounds for plants to survive. Some bacteria species can produce vitamins and help to support the human body's immune system. These bacteria and other useful microorganisms that are beneficial to mankind and the environment can be called the "good" microbes.

Some of the "good" microbes are useful in the treatment of soil and human bodies. However, the functions of many of the "good" bacteria have been overlooked by most Western researchers in the environmental and medical fields. Most agricultural industries do not study the use of nitrogen-fixing bacteria and fungi in soil health and crop production.   Probiotic bacteria are essential for the restoration of the microbe ecosystem in the human body, but most health professionals do not carry out research into their functions in repairing the system.

The study of "good" microbes in the environment and our bodies can be useful for us. Cyanobacteria and mycorrhizal fungi are two of the main groups of microbes that are essential for agriculture, and some probiotic species can be used to repair the human body. Research into these organisms can help to produce some fields in agriculture, environmental restoration, and medicine.

Why We Need to Study "Good" Bacteria in our Lives

    "Good" microbes, microorganisms that can be useful for our wellbeing, are essential for us and the environment. They help to contribute to these areas in our world, through their actions. Without these microbes, our environments and bodies would be dysfunctional. The "good" microbes can be studied for the restoration of the environment and human body.

    There are different kinds of "good" microbes that can be helpful for the environment and people. They can range from bacteria, fungi, to algae. The relationships between the "good" microbes and other organisms can be noticed for further studies. There are examples of mutualisms between some bacteria and fungi species, with plants and other "higher' organisms. In addition, there are some studies that help to show that some fungi species can help to remove toxic compounds from degraded soils and increase some crop yields. Many plant species depend upon fungi and bacteria for their growth. Some probiotic bacterial species can help to restore the microbial flora in the human body.

The environmental and medical fields are two of the research areas that the study of "good" microbes are needed. Many degraded ecosystems can be restored through the use of "good' bacteria and fungi. Some bacteria species can help to restore some of the organ functions in the human body. These organisms can be a good subject for further research in the environmental and medical fields. Therefore, the role of some microorganisms in their environment must be studied to carry out further research into their roles in restoration.

Microbes and their Role in the Environment

Many microorganisms help to play important roles in their environment, which are for the survival of many ecosystems on Earth. Most bacteria and fungi species served as decomposers, organisms that help to break down decaying matter into simple compounds that other creatures can used for their survival. Other bacteria species can use photosynthesis to covert gas into compounds that other organisms can used in their surroundings.   Their roles are needed from the health of many ecosystems, from the land to the oceans.

There are many kinds of microbes that help to provide benefits to their environment. They can be either bacteria, fungi, or algae. Many microbes are prokaryotic, organisms that do not have separate cell organelles. Bacteria are one of the main prokaryote organisms on Earth. Some microorganisms are eukaryotes, organisms that have recognized cell organelles such as a nucleus, chloroplast (plants and algae), and mitochondria. Fungi, algae, and other protists are classified as eukaryotes.

Some kinds of microorganisms are needed to be noticed for their contributions to the survival of living things. They can help to provide "higher" organisms nutrients and removal of toxic compounds in their environments.

Cyanobacteria and mycorrhizal fungi   are two of the many kinds of microorganisms that can be researched because they can help in the productivity of plants and other organisms in their environments. Their presence help to provide ecological balances to many organisms in their environments.   The study of cyanobacteria and mycorrhizal fungi can be a useful field for further research in helping to restore damaged ecosystems and increase productivity in agriculture.

Brief Notes about Cyanobacteria

Cyanobacteria are prokaryotic organisms that do not have major cell organelles such as a nucleus and chloroplast. However, they have chlorophyll and other pigments for their photosynthesis like many plants and algae. Many cyanobacteria species release oxygen through their photosynthesis. They can be found in many habitats on Earth, from the soil to the ocean.

There are many species of cyanobacteria, and they come in many forms. Some species are filamentous, while others have cells covered in gelatinous material. Some cyanobacteria species have the ability to fix nitrogen gas from the atmosphere into nitrate compounds that plants can used. Some filamentous cyanobacteria genus, such as *Anabaena*, can fix nitrogen through their heterocysts, special compartments in their cells that the enzyme nitrogenase is produced.

Cyanobacteria help to contribute their roles to many ecosystems on Earth. They can help to make conditions comfortable for other organisms in their environment. Many cyanobacteria species helped to form mats on the soil, which can accumulate soil particles over time. Some cyanobacteria species can help other plants to survive in their environments by providing nutrients and hormones for their growth. The cyanobacteria help to fix nitrogen compounds and secrete hormones for the plants' growth. *Anabaena* and *Nostoc* are some of the cyanobacteria genera that are known to form partnership with certain vascular plants such as rice (*Oryza sativa*) plants and *Azolla* water ferns. These cyanobacteria and other bacteria species are part of the microbial community in the plants' habitats. The plants contribute organic matter for the nearby bacteria to thrive in their habitats.

The presence of cyanobacteria in the environment has an impact on other organisms. Although many cyanobacteria species are known to form blooms that can affect nearby organisms in an aquatic ecosystem, there are some species that can be useful in research for environmental restoration. These organisms can help to clean degraded soils for other organisms to thrive. The fixing of nitrogen benefits many plants and other organisms in their environment.

Mycorrhizal Fungi and Plant Growth

Mycorrhizae are a group of fungi are associated with many plant species in helping to provide nutrients and hormones for their growth. They have the ability to transfer phosphorus and other nutrients to the plant host. In exchange, the plant provides the fungi with 20% carbon substances for their survival.   The fungi help to improve the plant's defense and stabilize the surrounding soil through the use of their hyphae and glomalin, a carbon-based compound that served to stabilize the surrounding soil, and as a carbon source for nearby organisms. The fungi do not harm the plant, but provide nutrients for their growth.

There are many kinds of mycorrhizal fungi that   form relationships with most plant species on Earth. Only a few plant families, such as Brassicaceae (Cabbage Family) and Caryophyllaceae (Pinks Family) do not associate with mycorrhizal fungi. Nevertheless, these fungi can have an impact on the productivity of a local, terrestrial ecosystem. Many mycorrhizal fungi are classified into two groups, the endomycorrhizal and ectomycorrhizal groups.

Endo mycorrhizal fungi are one of the most common types of fungi on Earth. They are able to produce their hyphae and fruiting bodies on the inside of the plant's roots. There are different kinds of endomycorrhizal fungi that associate with most plant species. The fungi binds to the roots, but the hyphae do not go pass the roots' cell walls. Arbuscular mycorrhizae is one of the common groups of fungi that associates with most plants such as grass and legumes. Ectomycorrhizal fungi have their fruiting bodies on the outside of many woody plant species, such as pine and maple trees. Like the endomycorrhizae fungi, ectomycorrhizal fungi' hyphae are attached to the hosts' roots. The fruiting bodies are formed on the outside of the hosts. Some of these species are the mushrooms that are familiar to many specialists.

These fungi are useful in helping to provide nutrients for plants and other organisms in the soil. Phosphorus is one of the macronutrients that plants and other microorganisms need for their survival. This element is needed to make nucleic acids and other cell structures. The phosphorus are needed by nitrogen fixing, purple bacteria in legumes. The bacteria helps to form nodules in the plants' roots. These nodules are the sites of nitrogen-fixation for the plants. Other plant species can be benefited by the presence of the mycorrhizal fungi in the environment. The material from the fungi can be used by other plant species during succession, the changing of a community over time.

The study of mycorrhizal fungi and cyanobacteria can be useful for many researchers in cleaning up degraded soils and improving crop yields in agriculture. Their roles can be researched through selected papers and books. Research into these organisms can help to cut cost in farm production and environmental clean-up of toxic soils.

Importance of Cyanobacteria and Fungi for Agriculture and Soil Cleanup

Cyanobacteria and mycorrhizal fungi are essential microorganisms for a healthy ecosystem, but the balance between them and their environment can be affected by excess chemicals and poor farming methods. Too much use of artificial fertilizers, herbicides, and other chemicals can affect plants and fungi relationships in the soil. The use of artificial fertilizers can alter the ecology of many of the microorganisms in the soil; thereby, allowing the decrease of nutrients and defense mechanisms to nearby plants. The excess runoff of nitrogen and phosphorous compounds from the fertilizers can cause an increase of cyanobacteria/ algae growth in the water that can affect many plants and animals in an aquatic ecosystem. Disturbance of the ground can alter mycorrhizal fungi network. Therefore, reintroducing cyanobacteria/mycorrhizal fungi into soil can be a useful idea for environmental scientists.

The study of the use of cyanobacteria and mycorrhizal fungi can be useful in restoring degraded soils from excess agriculture use. These organisms can help to return nutrients that the soil needs for its productivity. The studies of cyanobacteria and mycorrhizal fungi can be used to determine their effects on restoration of degraded soils. The use of these microorganisms can help cut down cost in fertilizer production for food production.

More energy is needed to produce artificial fertilizers than natural fertilizers. Petroleum and other materials are needed to produce artificial fertilizer for the farm. About 5% of the world's petroleum is needed to produce fertilizers for farmers and gardeners. The materials that are needed to produce fertilizers are costly to society and environment. Therefore, the study of cyanobacteria/mycorrhizal fungi is needed to help to create better growing conditions for crops and restoring degraded soil in the environment.

There have been studies on the use of cyanobacteria and mycorrhizal fungi to "clean" toxic soil and soil restoration. These organisms can be useful for "reviving" soil because they have the ability to absorb toxic metals and help to return nutrients to the surrounding environments.

Some cyanobacteria species are known to form soil mats that can hold carbon and nitrogen sinks that plants can grow in. In one experiment, some cyanobacteria species can help to improve conditions in some soil types. Two cyanobacteria species, *Phormidium ambiguum*, a non-nitrogen fixation, and *Scytonema javanicum* a N-fixing species, were used in a study of soil mat formation. The nitrogen-fixing species, *S. javanicum* had help to increase the carbon and nitrogen concentrations in the soil sample. *P. ambiguum* helped to stabilized many soil samples. The study of some species can be useful in restoring soil conditions for plant growth.

Some cyanobacteria and mycorrhizal fungi can be served as biofertilizers. Bio fertilizers are the production of plant nutrients through the use of microorganisms, in placed of artificial fertilizers. The byproducts from these organisms are used as nutrients that plants need for their growth. In India and other parts of the world, there had been studies of the use of cyanobacteria in the cultivation of some plant species such as rice (*Oryza sativa*) and wheat (*Triticum* spp). The researchers discovered that the plants have increased biomass when exposed in soils that contain cyanobacteria and associated bacteria. The cyanobacteria helps to produce nitrogen compounds, while the plant helps to provide nutrients for the aquatic community in the environment.

There has been research that helps to show that cyanobacteria and some fungi can help to remove toxic compounds from the soil. Some cyanobacteria species can produce extracelluar polymeric substances, polysaccride compounds that can bind on to some metals in their environment. Some mycorrhizal fungi have the ability to absorb metals in the soil, through their hyphae. Arbuscular mycorrhizae, one of the many kinds of endomycorrhizal fungi, produces glomalin, a carbon compound that helps to stabilize the soil and binds on to metals in the soil. Also, the fungi can use their hyphae to bind on to the metals in the soil. During the process, the fungi allows other microbes to settle in the soil. Mycorrhizal fungi are some of the groups of microbes that have been observed with soil samples in controlled conditions.

The use of cyanobacteria and mycorrhizal fungi to restore nutrients in the soil can be a needful field of research for many agricultural and environmental scientists. These organisms can help to increase crop yields, while helping to make the soil "healthy" for the plants and other organisms. Therefore, these "good" microbes can be useful in helping to determine ways of improving crop yield and providing better organic treatments for plants and soil conditions.

The study of "good" microbes in a terrestrial ecosystem can be reflected in the microbial community in the human body. The microbial community helps to form a balanced ecosystem in the human body. There are many kinds of bacteria that inhabited the human body, and they can perform different functions in the body, from defense to vitamin production. Therefore, the study of the microbial ecosystem in the human body is needed to be an important field in medicine.

The Importance of "Good "Microbes in the Human Body

The human body is one of the living systems in which a microbial ecosystem can be found. In our bodies, there are billions of bacteria and other microbes that perform several functions that are needed for the system. Some bacterial species have the ability to produce acidic conditions that repel other microorganisms in our bodies. Others can produce enzymes that help to convert complex molecules into simple compounds for metabolism. Some bacteria species are known to produce vitamins for our bodies.

However, excess treatment for infections and cancer can cause an imbalance of the microbial community in the body. Antibiotics are good to remove harmful bacteria from the body, but the microbial system needs to be replenish for the body to be functioned. If the patient's body depends upon antibiotics along, then the microbial system will be out of balance. Also, some of the populations of the bad bacteria will become resistant to the antibiotic. The use of reintroducing "good" bacteria into a patient can be studied to improve the body's system. The "good" bacteria can be used to restore the body's microbial ecosystem.   The use of probiotics can be one of the solutions in helping to restore a patient's microbial community after treatment.

Probiotics are "good" bacteria that made of species that can be found in the digestive tract. They are useful in helping to restore the body's function. Most of the useful bacteria genera that are used in most probiotic foods can be found in our intestines. *Lactobacilli* and *Bifidobacteria* are two of the most known kinds of "good" bacteria genera that help to make up the gastrointestinal community. *Lactobacilli* are found in the small intestines, while *Bifidobacteria* is found in the large intestines. Some *Lactobacilli* species can help to produce lactase, an enzyme that helps to convert lactose into simple sugars for the body. *Bifidobacteria* is known to produce conditions that other bacteria species cannot tolerate. This includes making lactic and acetic acid in the intestines that can lower the pH of its environment.

The use of probiotics can be one way to restore the microbial system in a patient, but caution must be taken for this medicine. Taking too many probiotics can help to cause an infection. Nevertheless, probiotic bacteria species can be a start to help to restore a patient's health after treatment.

The Conclusion of the Matter

There are several kinds of "good" microbes that can be beneficial for us and the environment. Some kinds can be decomposers and producers in their environments. Some bacteria species, such as cyanobacteria and purple bacteria are needed to produce nutrients for the growth of many plant species. Other microbes can be useful in helping to remove toxic metals from soils; thereby, helping to improve the lives of other organisms in that environment.

The use of "good" microbes in our lives can be observed in the field or a lab condition. The study of these organisms can be useful for many researchers. There are some examples of the types and benefits of certain microbes in the environment and our bodies. Cyanobacteria, mycorrhizal fungi, and probiotic bacteria are some of microorganisms that can be useful in reviving the environment and our bodies. The study of cyanobacteria and mycorrhizal fungi can be useful for researching how to reintroduce "good' microbes into toxic soils. These organisms can help to transform the soil for plants. *Lactobacilli, Bifidobacteria,* and other probiotic bacteria genera can help to replenish a patient's body after treatment.   Like restoring soil health, the human body needs certain microbes for survival.

There are ways to reintroduce these organisms to damaged systems. They can be introduce as active cultures to an environment. Researchers can observed how these organisms can interact with a barren environment to restart an ecosystem. Therefore, the study of these organisms can help to reduce costs for treatment of the ecosystem and the human body. The study of these microbes can help to form new fields of study for many scientists. There had been researchers in many areas of the world that study the effects of "good" microbes on plants and humans.

There are many published papers on the use of microorganisms for biofertilizers in the soil and probiotics for the human body. These papers can be searched through online sites and paper journals. These papers can be a useful for support for further research. Nevertheless, we can turn to God to give us understanding about these microbes.

How to Contact the Author

You can contact the author through email: grasshopper_60619@yahoo.com

References

Abdul G, Khan. Mycorrhizoremediation-an enhanced form of phytoremediation. Journal of Zhejiang University SCIENCE B. 2006 7(7):503-514.

Carr, N.G. and BA Whitton. Botanical Monographs, Vol 9: The Biology of Blue-Green Algae. University of California Press. Berkeley and Los Angeles. 1973.

Chamizo, Sonia et al. Cyanobacteria Inoculation Improves Soil Stability and Fertility on Different Textured Soils: Gaining Insights for Applicability in Soil Restoration: Frontiers in Environmental Science. Vol 6:49. 2018.

DeSalle Rob, Susan L. Perkins, and Patricia J. Wynne. Welcome to the Microbiome. Yale University Press. New Haven. 2015.

Fay, Peter. The Institute of Biology's Studies in Biology no. 160. The Blue-Greens (Cyanophyta-Cyanobacteria). Edward Arnold; Baltimore. 1983.

Heavy Metals and Cyanobacteria: Towards Bioremediation. Atlas of Science:

      Another View on Science. Website.

Huffnagle, Gary B. Sarah Wernick. The Probiotic Revolution. Bantam Books. 2007.

Latta, Sara L. and Dennis Kunkel, Ph.D. The Good, The Bad, The Slimy: The Secret
Life of Microbes. Enslow Publishers, Inc. Berkeley Heights. 2006.

Lowerfels, Jeff. Teaming with Fungi: The Organic Grower's Guide to Mycorrhizae.

Timber Press. Portland. 2017.

------------- Teaming with Nutrients: The Organic Gardener's Guide to Optimizing
Plant Nutrition. Timber Press, Portland. 2013.

Prasanna, Radha et al. Cyanobacterial diversity in the rhizosphere of rice and its
ecological significance. Indian Journal of Microbiology. 49: 89-97. 2009.

Stephenson, Steven L. The Kingdom Fungi: The Biology of Mushrooms, Molds, and
Lichens. Timber Press; Portland. 2010.

The Truth about Phosphates and Mycorrhizal Fungi. LebanonTurf Website.

      13 May 2013.

Trener, Natasha. Probiotics: Nature's Internal Healers. Avery Publishing Group; Garden City Park. 1998.